FOREWORD

I never enter St Marie's without marvelling at the vision, courage and faith of the young priest, Fr Charles Pratt, who commissioned it. Only two years previously John Henry Newman had become a Catholic; the hierarchy had not yet been re-established; and Fr Pratt was only 35 years old.

I feel proud too that the architect was a Sheffield man, Charles Hadfield, who designed surely one of the finest neo-Gothic churches.

My first association with this lovely church was on 25 January 1968 when I was consecrated bishop here. Twelve years later on 3 July 1980 I was enthroned as the first Bishop of Hallam. Between these two events great and necessary alterations took place. This was magnificently done in 1973 under the guidance of Mgr Stephen Sullivan and by the skill of Mr Jimmy Frame (RIP). The result is a beautiful and open sanctuary with an unimpeded view of the glorious east window. Thus St Marie's was perfectly fitted to become the Cathedral that it had so clearly been designed to be.

11 September 1989 is the Centenary of the Consecration of St Marie's. As it has done in the past may it continue to glorify God and, through the intercession of Mary to whom it is dedicated, elevate the mind and heart of everyone who comes to pray.

Gerald Moverley

Bishop of Hallam

Acknowledgements

A short history of St Marie's was written by the Right Reverend Monsignor S.P. Sullivan.

The *Guide to St Marie's*, based on that of Mrs A. Hemphill, was revised by the Reverend J. Ryan, who would like to thank Mr W. Burleigh, Dr P. Howell, and the Reverend Dr J. Sharp for their assistance.

First published in 1988 by
Fowler Wright Books
Burgess Street, Leominster
Herefordshire

☆

☆

Typesetting by Print Origination (NW) Limited, Formby, Liverpool L37 8EG
Printed and bound in Great Britain by
Clifford Frost Limited, Wimbledon, London SW19 2ST

A SHORT HISTORY OF ST MARIE'S

1. *Following the Reformation*

At the time of the Reformation Sheffield was a small place. The Parish Church (now the Cathedral of St Peter and St Paul) went over to the new Protestant faith, and Catholics were outlawed and had no place for Mass. On 12 July 1588, at Padley just fifteen miles from Sheffield, two priests, Nicholas Garlick and Robert Ludlum, were arrested for saying Mass. They were executed at Derby on 24 July the same year.

Through the seventeenth and well into the eighteenth century, towns were dangerous places for Catholics to gather, so Mass was celebrated in homes in country districts. A signal, perhaps a white sheet on a bush, was given when Mass was to be said. Fulwood Hall, at that time belonging to the Fox family, was one such home. Nethergate Hall in Stannington (later to become the site of St Mary's School) which belonged to the Revell family was another. When Rowland Revell died without marrying in 1742, the Catholic centre moved to Revell Grange where his younger brother Thomas lived. Here the special Mass Room with alcove for altar, recess for confessional and direct stairway to the outside of the house can still be seen. Thomas' only daughter married Richard Broomhead and they became the leading Catholic family in the district. Their daughter Teresa married Thomas Wright and inherited Revell Grange.

When St Marie's was built in 1850, Teresa Wright donated the stained glass window in the South wall of the South Transcept. The first panel depicts her patron, St Teresa of Avila, and Teresa Wright herself is shown kneeling at the saint's feet.

As the eighteenth century progressed, Catholics were able to move back into the towns and celebrate Mass and the Sacraments more openly. In August 1728 Bishop Williams (Vicar Apostolic of the Northern District) confirmed sixty-two people in the Chapel of the "Lord's House". This was a large house built on the corner of Norfolk Row, with a large garden. Attached to the house was a chapel large enough to hold three hundred people. The house was the home of Henry Howard, Agent to the Duke of Norfolk. There was a resident priest on his staff who had charge of the Sheffield Mission.

At the time of the Bishop's Visitation, Ignatius Brookes S.J. was in charge. He moved to Spinkhill and secular clergy took over. Christopher Gradwell, newly ordained from the College at Douai in France took up residence on 11 October 1736. He served the people of Sheffield until his death in 1758. He was succeeded by John Lodge who asked for an assistant, so large had the mission grown. His first assistant was William Winter who stayed until 1775. He was followed by Rowland Broomhead who had been born at Revell Grange and was educated at the Venerable English College, Rome. There he had distinguished himself by a brilliant academic record which caused him to be chosen to deliver an oration before the Pope (Clement XIV). He stayed for three years before moving to Lancashire where he established Churches in Manchester and Bolton. Samuel Sayles came in his place and became Rector when Lodge moved to Durham. He was followed by Richard Rimmer who arrived in 1787.

Rev. Rowland Broomhead

2. Change and growth

Until the passing of the First Relief Act in 1778, which repealed some of the penal laws against Catholics, a Catholic priest could be imprisoned indefinitely, as could a Catholic teacher for running a school, no Catholic could own or inherit land. Although these laws were seldom invoked they remained on the Statute Book. Their repeal caused the infamous Gordon Riots in London, but the furore soon died down. Further relaxation of the laws came with the Toleration Act of 1791. A priest could now openly exercise his ministry; Catholics could own property, and therefore build churches.

During the second half of the eighteenth century, Sheffield was becoming an industrial town. In 1740 if you crossed Lady's Bridge you were in the country. Parkhill was a grassy slope. The Moor really was a moor. Broomhall was a mansion a good way out of the town. The population was densely packed in Market Place, Snig Hill and Water Lane, and in a maze of Crofts and Alley-ways in a fan from Pinstone Street, West Street, and Trippet Lane down to West Bar. The invention of crucible steel by Benjamin Huntsman and the discovery of a better way of plating copper with silver made it possible for cutlery companies to open up foreign trade. Suddenly the town was bursting.

In 1814 Vincent Eyre, the Agent to the Duke of Norfolk, was anxious to move from the crowded town centre and put the Lord's House on the market. Richard Rimmer rallied his flock to raise money to buy the house and retain their chapel. The enthusiasm for the project was enormous, and an even more ambitious scheme was planned. Not only would they raise the cash to buy the chapel and the land adjoining it, but they would build a bigger and better chapel on the site. The project was completed within an astonishing two years, and there was a solemn opening in May 1816. The Sheffield "Iris" newspaper commented:

> On Wednesday last, the new Catholic Chapel lately erected in Norfolk Row, was opened by the celebration of High Mass, and an eloquent and impressive sermon delivered by the Rev. P. Baines to a crowded audience.

A reminiscence of the Lord's House and Richard Rimmer was published in 1875 in *Reminiscences of Old Sheffield, Its Streets and Its People* (edited by Robert Eadon Leader):

> At the end of Norfolk row, opposite the old Cutlers' Arms, was the building called the old Lord's House. It formed the corner of Fargate and Norfolk row, and stood where are the shop so long occupied by Mr Holden, watchmaker (now Mr Rennie's, hosier), and the adjacent ones, as far as the 'Old Red House'. There was a double flight of steps, leading to a balcony on the level of the first floor. Mr Rimmer, the Catholic priest, had a small room in the house, used as a chapel. The entrance was from the Norfolk row side, and there were two or three steps up to the chapel. About the time I am speaking of (1815), the building was taken down, and the land was quite open from Fargate to the Assembly Rooms in Norfolk St, and it continued open for years. Mr Rimmer got a chapel built upon the ground, right at the back (1816), and that continued to be the Roman Catholic place of worship until the present St Marie's Church was built (1846-50). We used to play on the ground, and 'Old Rimmer' did not like it and drove us off. He was a nice old gentleman—'a cheerful old chap'. For a long time the ground was unfenced, but ultimately a palisade was put up. (p.265)

Richard Rimmer died on Monday 12 May 1828 very suddenly, aged 73. He had served in Sheffield for over forty years. The *Sheffield Register* reporting his death, said that he had not left an enemy behind him.

Rev. Charles Pratt

3. Fr Charles Pratt and plans for a new church

After Richard Rimmer's death a number of priests took charge of the Sheffield Mission in quick succession until in November 1843 Charles Joseph Pratt was appointed Rector. He was in his early thirties and full of enthusiasm for the Gothic revival that was sweeping the country. Spacious churches were being built in all the growing towns. Fr Pratt began by cleaning and renovating the Chapel built twenty-five years earlier by Richard Rimmer. The full splendour of the Roman Liturgy was established. The Rosminian Dr Gentili preached a Mission and there was a real spirit of renewal among the Catholics of Sheffield.

In 1845 the property alongside the chapel was purchased for £1,400 and the possibility of building a beautiful Gothic church was announced. With the visit of Bishop Briggs in 1846 to confirm two hundred and ninety people the scheme was launched. In a short time £5,300 was raised. Fr Pratt negotiated for the use of the unoccupied Mount Tabor Methodist church as an interim Catholic chapel. On Sunday 10 January 1847 Fr Pratt preached for the last time in the Norfolk Row Chapel. On the following Saturday Bishop Briggs dedicated the Mount Tabor Chapel in honour of St John the Baptist, and Mass was celebrated the following day. The Chapel in Norfolk Row was demolished and the site prepared for the new Church. Work began on the foundations for the new Church on Candlemass day, 2 February, and the corner-stone was laid on the Feast of the Annunciation, 25 March 1847 by Bishop Briggs. The architect mainly involved in the work was Matthew Ellison Hadfield, the young partner of John Gray Weightman.

Of all M.E. Hadfield's works, St Marie's is surely a masterpiece. The design was based on a study of fourteenth-century churches in Yorkshire and Lincolnshire, especially St Andrew's, Heckington. The style is a rich and flowing decorated. The building was much praised at its completion. Eastlake in his *History of the Gothic Revival* (1872) considered it 'a model of excellence'.

Part of the site was graveyard, therefore the bodies had to be respectfully removed. Fr Pratt supervised the transfer to the nearest Catholic cemetery, St Bede's in Rotherham. During this operation Fr Pratt, who never enjoyed good health, caught a chill which lingered for twelve months. He was nevertheless able to take a keen interest in the growing new building. Then in the January of 1849 his health deteriorated rapidly. He died on the evening of 17 February, aged 38 years.

Fr Pratt was buried in St Bede's churchyard. However, the stonemason building the new church, Benjamin Gregory, who was not a Catholic, had other ideas. He had got to know Fr Pratt well and had often heard him say that he would like his tomb to be in the church. As the building progressed, the mason built a tomb on the northside of the Sanctuary. In the dead of night on 24th March, he took a few friends to Rotherham and secretly disinterred the coffin, bringing it back to Sheffield on a dray in the early hours of the morning. He hid the dray in his yard in Portobello until the evening when he brought the coffin to church and placed it in the tomb he had prepared. When the church was opened an effigy was designed, said to be a good likeness of the priest, and placed above Fr Pratt's final resting place.

During the re-ordering of the church in 1971, the effigy was transferred to the Mortuary Chapel. When the new sanctuary floor was being laid, the coffin of Fr Pratt was seen, intact, resting on a brick pedestal. It was left undisturbed. A plaque on the sanctuary wall testifies to the presence of Fr Pratt's remains.

In August 1849 Fr William Parsons came to Sheffield. He was a man of large ideas. He decided to erect a spire, and had more elaborate work done on altars and screens than was originally intended. He stayed less than a year and was succeeded by Fr Edmund Scully.

The date for the solemn opening of the church was fixed for

Wednesday 11 September. Quietly on the Tuesday morning Bishop Briggs consecrated the High Altar and celebrated the first Mass. The Dedication Service was fixed for 11.00am the next day. Entry to the church was by ticket and there were a thousand of them. Those without a ticket gathered in Norfolk Row to watch the arrivals and the procession. The Earl and Countess of Arundel were there as were many other Catholic gentry from around the country. The Church procession was impressive—led by two abbots, Westminster and Mount St Bernard; then came the Bishops, Bishop Brown from Wales, Bishop Waring from the Eastern district, Bishop Gillis from Scotland, Bishop Morris from Mauritius, and Archbishop Nakar from the Lebanon. Finally came Bishop Briggs of Yorkshire who was to celebrate the Mass. Bishop Gillis preached for an hour. A Miss Whitnall from Liverpool sang a Motet 'in an exquisite manner'. The Earl of Arundel took the collection which raised three hundred pounds. The ceremony ended with a solemn 'Te Deum'.

Another packed congregation attended an evening service at which Bishop Morris preached. The following morning the Archbishop of the Lebanon said Mass in Syriac at 7.00am. Bishop Morris consecrated the altar in the Blessed Sacrament Chapel, and the Abbot of Mount St Bernard said Mass in the Norfolk Chapel (St Joseph's) in the presence of the Earl and Countess of Arundel. At half past ten a full church heard a solemn dirge sung in memory of Fr Pratt.

The following Sunday Fr Faber from the Brompton Oratory preached a sermon about our Blessed Lady, making a deep impression on the congregation.

Among the clergy present on these occasions was a Fr Robert Cornthwaite from Stockton. He was to become the first Bishop of Leeds.

The cost of building the Church was as follows:

	£	s	d
Masonry and plastering	5,335	5	7½
Carpentry and joinery	1,869	19	5
Stone carving	520	3	6
High Altar Screen and Tabernacle	278	17	9
Ironwork and Gasfitting, Hot Air Apparatus	511	1	3
Benches and Chairs	223	0	0
Plumbing, painting, glazing	444	14	5½
Slating	318	11	2
Copper wire &c	74	1	3
Bulmer—Chancel Roof	100	0	0
Monumental Brass	17	17	0
Mears—for Bell	139	0	0
Law bills	186	0	0
Architects	450	0	0
Clerk of Works	88	3	6
One year's Insurance	5	17	3
Total	£10,562	12	2

In addition to this are the windows, which were given and cost about £750.

4. Canon Scully

Two weeks after the opening of St Marie's, Pope Pius IX, re-established diocesan bishops in England and Wales. There was to be one Archbishop (at Westminster) and twelve suffragan bishops. The whole of Yorkshire became the Diocese of Beverley with Bishop Briggs as its first Bishop. Among the Canons in the new Cathedral Chapter was Fr Scully, the parish priest at St Marie's.

Soon after St Marie's was opened, the suggestion was made to Canon Scully that some guilding and decoration should be added to the panelled ceiling of the Blessed Sacrament Chapel. His reply was a firm "No. We must first of all guild a few souls in White Croft".

White Croft was an area of Sheffield around West Bar, where the Irish immigrants fleeing the potato famine had settled. They were desperately poor, living in overcrowded conditions with little sanitation, and the victims of rivalry and bigotry; an embarrassment, it seems, to the native Catholics of the town.

In April 1851 some land was bought by a mortgage at the top of White Croft, and by 1853 a school building had been erected with the help of a government grant. Meanwhile, Canon Scully had been negotiating with the Provincial of the Vincentian Fathers at Castleknock who agreed to send some of his priests to Sheffield. Frs Michael Burke, Thomas Plunkett and James Kelly with a lay-brother John Bradley arrived at the beginning of November to take up residence at 90 Garden St. On the first Sunday of Advent Fr Burke said Mass in the new school which was to double as the Parish Church. He described that first morning:

> The morning was cold, the room was scarcely half filled by a badly dressed, poor, perished looking congregation. This beginning was not very encouraging.

But he stayed and lived to see a thriving parish grow.

Canon Scully also saw the need of help in the schools of the town and approached the Sisters of Notre Dame de Namur. On 25 July 1855 four sisters left Liverpool for Sheffield. One of the sisters described their journey:

> We left Liverpool on a Wednesday morning, taking our route through Manchester, where we had to change trains. It was raining fast and we had only five minutes. Sister Ursula carried in her arms a statue of our Blessed Lady which she would allow no one to take from her. We had been a little more than an hour in the train when we were told that all the passengers had to leave the carriage, as the tunnel was being repaired and we could not go through. In the pouring rain we had to climb up a steep embankment and get into omnibuses waiting for us at the top. These drove us to the other end of the tunnel, about five miles, when we had to walk down another embankment to enter a train again. When we got to Sheffield there was no one to meet us; we drove about the town for some time, not knowing the address of our future convent, and asking for St Marie's Church.

The new Convent was Holy Green House on the Moor. Within two weeks the sisters were working in St Vincent's school and a week later in St Marie's school while at the same time establishing a Day and Boarding School for the young ladies of Sheffield in Holy Green House. The sisters made a great impression, as the local press commented:

> They frequently appear in the streets, and the novelty of their costume attracts much attention.

The Sisters required more extensive accommodation within a few years and in 1861 purchased a large property just off the Glossop Road. It was situated by the Public Baths and bordered by, as coincidence would have it, 'Convent Walk'. This became the Convent and a Ladies' Boarding School. After the Great War, more property had to be acquired. In February 1919 'Oakbrook' on the Fulwood Road, formerly the residence of the Firth Family, was bought to house the sisters and the boarders.

5. Fr William Fisher

Fr William Fisher, a native of Blackburn, replaced Canon Scully in 1855. He had been educated at Ushaw College, County Durham, and had taught there for a few years after his ordination. He came to Sheffield after a short period as a curate at St Wilfred's, York. He faced an urgent problem with the parish debt which had grown with the expansion of recent years. He was a man of business. He organised a weekly outdoor collection, urging everyone to give according to their needs. The Duke of Norfolk undertook to treble the amount subscribed by the congregation. By 1866 a massive £3,000 had been raised.

Despite the debt, Canon Fisher did not hesitate to spend when more building was needed. St Marie's School in Surrey Street, had become inadequate for the needs of the parish. The Duke of Norfolk gave some land opposite the farm grounds and along Sheaf Gardens (now the roundabout at the bottom of Granville Road). Here a new school for girls was built with the sisters of Notre Dame in charge. The school remained in use until it was bombed during the Second World War.

A school and chapel-of-ease was established in 1863 in Lee Croft (now part of the bus-depot at the bottom of Townhead Street). The Old Lee Croft Independent Chapel was purchased through intermediaries, altered, and opened on 11 January by the new Bishop of Beverley, Bishop Cornthwaite. The chapel was dedicated to St William. The sisters of Notre Dame ran the school.

In 1864 the population of Sheffield was spreading eastwards. Canon Fisher obtained a site in Salmon Pastures and built a temporary chapel. It was dedicated to St Catherine, though it later became the parish of St Charles in Attercliffe.

Canon Fisher resigned due to ill-health in 1866 and went away for a period of convalescence. This seems to have been successful since he was appointed to the Bridlington parish where he served until his death in 1886 when he was 74.

Canon Samuel Walshaw

6. Canon Samuel Walshaw

Samuel Walshaw was his successor. After studying at Ushaw, he was ordained in 1852, serving at Barnard Castle and Wycliffe before coming to Sheffield. One of his first acts was to arrange for the Angelus to be rung morning, noon and night. A great revival in plain-chant as the proper music for the liturgy was underway. This was to be sung by choir, dressed in surplices, in the sanctuary. Until this time the organ and choir were situated in a gallery above the West door. Now the organ was moved to the north side of the Chancel (where it is today). The 'new music' was inaugurated at the Midnight Mass of 1870. The gallery was eventually removed.

At a mission preached in Lent 1870 by Fr J. Clare S.J. it was decided to establish a Council of the St Vincent de Paul Society, affiliated to the Head Council recently formed in Paris. From that day to the present, the Society has cared for the needy of the parish and area.

The social mission of the Church was also promoted by establishing a home for needy girls—St Joseph's at Howard Hill. This was run by the Sisters of Charity until it closed in 1978.

The Sisters of Charity also ran a school for the deaf. This was established in Handsworth Woodhouse. All the Bishops took an interest and decided a larger establishment was needed. So in 1875 the sisters with forty-seven pupils left Handsworth for Boston Spa, outside Leeds, where the school went from strength to strength and enjoys today a national, if not international, reputation.

The needs of the aged poor were also answered when the Little Sisters of the Poor came to 80 Duchess Rd.

At this time the Duke of Norfolk lived in Sheffield, and through his continuing generosity parishes were set up in the growing areas of the town. In 1871 a chapel was established in Handsworth, and ten years later the Duke built a church there.

In 1875 a school was built under his direction in Andover Square with a room large enough to double as a Church. Fr Luke Burke was appointed as Parish Priest. He felt the need of a community of nuns to help in the school and to visit the poor of the parish. He went to London to try and persuade the Sisters of Mercy to come to Sheffield. An account of what followed was kept by one of the sisters:

> The Rev. L. Burke called late on 14 December 1882 to see could he get a foundation from 535 Commercial Road to teach his children. We had a good laugh, thinking it was a castle in the air, not having one Sister to spare from our own schools. I know not how it came to pass—it seems a mystery still; our ecclesiastical superiors thought two sisters might be spared. On 2 May 1883 Sister Mary Vincent Flanaghan and Sister Scholastica McDonald, with Miss Lucas started by the 10.10 train from the Great Northern and arrived at Sheffield where we were met by his reverence and conducted to the presbytery dinner awaiting us.

These sisters moved into 92 Andover St., and soon the community numbered six sisters. The parish also grew under the patronage of St Catherine. Thus began a long and continuing association of the Sisters of Mercy with Sheffield. In 1921 the Claremont Nursing Home was opened in Claremont Crescent, moving to Sandygate Lane in 1953.

By 1879 the number of Catholics in the Sharrow, Healy and Highfield area warranted attention. Again the Duke responded. He provided a site "surrounded on every side by streets, and erected, at a cost of £10,000, schools for eight hundred children, fitted with every modern convenience." This was St Wilfred's which stood until German bombs destroyed it in the Second World War.

After the building of the girls' schools at Sheaf Gardens, the Surrey Street School was used by the boys. This was now too small. Yet again the Duke's generosity was shown. Once a site had been bought in Edmund Road, the Duke paid for a new school to accommodate four hundred boys and a master's house. On the appointed day, all the boys were lined up in Surrey Street and, led by a band, they marched down the Moor and St Mary's Gate to take up residence in their new school. It was festival day for all.

7. The consecration

By 1880 the Church had been opened for thirty years and had not yet been consecrated. Church Law forbade a Church to be consecrated until it was free of debt, and £4,000 was still owing on St Marie's. Despite the expansion of churches and schools in the city, Canon Walshaw was determined to witness the consecration ceremony. A concerted effort was made to raise the money. Times were hard and there were many other calls made on precious resources. Nevertheless at the Sunday evening service on 22 September 1888, the Canon solemnly announced that the Church was free of debt. A 'Te Deum' was sung in thanksgiving by the whole congregation. During the following Lent a mission was preached for two weeks by the Servite Fathers, and so began the spiritual preparation for the great event.

No account of the ceremony remains, nor is the date of it known, other than that it was in early September. The ceremony is a long and elaborate one, in which the Bishop anoints twelve crosses placed around the inside wall; below these crosses candle-holders are fixed and these candles are lit on the anniversary which was fixed by the Bishop as 11 September, the date of the Church opening in 1850.

By 1896 the Canon had been Parish Priest at St Marie's for thirty years. He had seen the town expand greatly, and the Mother Parish had given birth to many daughters. He was well-known and respected by all. He was now sixty years of age. As Holy Week approached it was clear he was not well. A priest from Spinkhill was to come and help with the ceremonies, but had to cancel at the last minute. The Canon decided he would celebrate the events of Holy Week himself. Palm Sunday almost proved too much and it was clear to the people that their priest was very ill. He managed the other ceremonies however, and on Easter Sunday preached at the High Mass in the morning and at Solemn Vespers in the evening two very moving sermons on the Resurrection. The next day he collapsed; by Tuesday he was unconscious. He died during the night, just as his relatives from Scarborough arrived. The following morning both Sheffield papers had glowing accounts of his life. One concluded:

His was wholehearted devotion to his Church. To it his death will be a severe blow, and his loss as a citizen will be felt by all sections of the community.

Canon Walshaw was remembered by an old boy of St Marie's school in Edmund Road:

Being now a St Edmund's boy I was expected to attend Sunday School, and so, Sunday after Sunday found me sitting with the boys in St Marie's Church, boys on the Gospel side, girls on the epistle side. In the middle aisle, sitting in an armchair facing the children, the Very Rev. Canon Samuel Walshaw, a copy of the catechism in his hand. He questioned boys and girls in turn, breaking down the answers to our understanding, stressing the virtues, Truth, Honesty, Good Manners etc. These Sunday afternoons remain my first strong memory of St Marie's, never forgotten; and the venerable saintly priest, whose body now rests in City Road Cemetery near the gate in Manor Lane.

Canon William Gordon

8. Canon Oswald Dolan

In 1890 Bishop Cornthwaite, who had been Bishop of Leeds for nearly thirty years, asked the Pope to appoint a coadjutor Bishop to assist him. Early in February Fr William Gordon was consecrated Bishop and succeeded Bishop Cornthwaite who died in June of that year. At the death of Canon Walshaw, the Bishop sent his brother as the new Parish Priest. In that year, 1896, the Duke of Norfolk was Mayor and the following year he was Lord Mayor, for the town had become a city. The Town Hall was completed and Queen Victoria came to open it, however, she was too weak to get out of the carriage and the Duke did the honours. In both years the Civic Service was Sunday High Mass in St Marie's. Canon Gordon, who was remembered as a stern man, found he could not settle in Sheffield, and after only two years he asked to be moved and was transferred to Harrogate.

Canon Oswald Dolan

And so in 1898 Fr Oswald Dolan came to Sheffield. He was destined to be the longest serving priest at St Marie's, staying until his death thirty-seven years later.

One of his first acts was to close the Chapel of St William at Lee Croft, which was a short distance from St Marie's and even less from St Vincent's. Though the name was to be preserved in the parish soon to be founded in Ecclesall.

Plans for the celebration of St Marie's golden jubilee were soon put in hand. Plainsong was now out of fashion. The great composer of church music was Dom Perosi in Rome. So Mr Lawrence the organist and choirmaster prepared for the great day by rehearsing the latest three-part Mass. The event was celebrated on Tuesday 11 September in the presence of a great assembly of clergy, the Bishop of Leeds and the Duke of Norfolk. History does not record the preacher but he must have been a little long-winded because the Bishop fell asleep. As the Morning Telegraph reported the next day:

> The Roman Catholic Bishop of Leeds . . . candidly confessed that he had gone to sleep during the sermon preached earlier in the day. The Bishop is sensible enough to dislike long luncheons, long speeches, and long sermons. (The Bishop was speaking at a luncheon at the Cutler's Hall). What is more, the Bishop is courageous enough to say so. The Lord Mayor of Sheffield, who was amongst the guests, made tactful and spirited reference to the reappearance in our midst of the Duke of Norfolk, after serving his country at the front. (This was presumably a reference to the Boer war.)

In 1905 a plot of land was obtained and a chapel built to serve the growing number of people in the Ecclesall area. This was given the title of St William of York.

Until the end of the nineteenth century the priests at St Marie's lived in the house at the end of Norfolk Row which now houses the Coventry Building Society. It is still called 'Rectory Chambers' and had been owned by Sir Arnold Knight, a well-known doctor of the town. In 1902 the land behind the Church was vacated and Dean Dolan purchased it to build a new presbytery which would be linked to the Church and provided much needed space for vesting, for choir practise and for meetings.

Dean Dolan also bought the Baptist chapel in Townhead Street and this doubled as a parish hall and men's club until it was taken over during the Second World War and used as a canteen for the engineering works next door. It was demolished in 1979.

At the outbreak of the First World War, the Dean, though not a young man, was one of the first to volunteer. He served with distinction in the ill-fated Gallipoli expedition and in France. He was mentioned in Despatches in 1917 and decorated by the Portuguese Government with the Order of Christ for his services to wounded Portuguese troops.

On the clear moonlit night of 26 September 1916, at 11.00pm a zeppelin flew over Sheffield, a beautiful and fearsome sight. It seemed to move away and everyone went to bed. Then, at 2.00am there was the sound of bombs falling. One house in Cassey St. was destroyed and several people were killed near Norfolk Bridge on Attercliffe Road. People had been assured that full defensive arrangements had been made, but only one shell was fired from the defensive post in Manor Lane, and the cap of that shell was found a few days later on Wincobank Hill. After this the streets were darkened.

A life-long parishioner of St Marie's, Hazel Worth, who was a pupil in the girls' school at Sheaf Gardens was just ten when war broke out. She remembers:

The fact that the Dean became a chaplain to the forces filled us with awe and admiration, and certainly our school life was dominated with the awareness of the sacrifices made by the Dean and our soldiers in the trenches. We visualized them as daily being shot by the Germans, and our half-pennies and pennies pocket money were solemnly donated for Mass offerings for their safe return. The Dean's portrait in khaki held the place of honour over Sister's desk in the middle-room, and we brought our newspapers and magazines for Sister to send to France and the Dean to distribute among the boys. We wrote letters full of all the trivia of school and Church news; and he in his turn would send a postcard to each person who wrote to him.

Whenever he came home on leave there was great excitement. A 'big girl' would be posted outside school to look along Suffolk Road, and then return breathlessly to report 'He's coming—he's nearly here'. Goodness me! The clapping and the cheering which broke out on his arrival, and the loud 'Hoorays' which drowned the Dean's laughter. There was tea and buns and sweets for everyone, and of course, the inevitable concert. I remember how we sang to the tune of 'Tipperary':

'Twas a long way to Gallipoli,
Twas a long way to go;
Twas a long way to Gallipoli,
But you went there we know.
Just to teach us, your little children,
That hard things must be done,
For our dear Lord, our King and Captain
said, 'Tis thus crowns are won.'

When he did come home for good, there was a formal welcome in the Hall, and a presentation and illuminated address, with an announcement from Bishop Cowgill, Bishop of Leeds, that our Dean was to be 'Canon Dolan'; and I remember feeling a slight disappointment as I thought the new title didn't slip half as euphoniously from the tongue as the much loved 'Dean Dolan'!

All was not misery in Sheffield in the war for it was a boom town owing to the heavy war-time demand for steel. Vickers' annual output of guns increased from three hundred to three thousand; Firths and Cammells turned out a million shells each. Steel, Peech and Tozers extended their plane considerably. Plenty of money was being made. The workers were determined to get their share of the boom and went on strike for more pay. Canon Dolan was indignant. "When I came away from France," he said, "the men were talking freely about these strikers, and were very sarcastic about them. The wounded men are particularly emphatic in their opinions, and in contrasting the position of the strikers with themselves. They get 1/6d a day risking their lives in the trenches, whilst these men get £5 or £6 a week living in safety at home. There are plenty of skilled men in the army who feel that it is the turn of some of these men who have been earning big wages to take some of the risk, and let the men in the trenches have a rest." This was in the July of 1918 and the Canon was convinced that the war would last a long time yet. He was wrong. The end came suddenly and with it a slump. In 1921 there was another coal strike, and that year the number of unemployed rose to 69,300. In June and August there were demonstrations by the unemployed, leading to threats, broken windows, and near riots.

Yet despite the depression the work of the Church expanded. In 1923 the Canon secured the establishment of De La Salle College to provide for Catholic boys an education similar to that provided for the girls for over eighty years at Notre Dame. In that same year the men's society known as the Knights of St Columba was established. The knights meet for their own spiritual growth, to help the Catholic community at large, and to give some Catholic voice in the life of the city. This year also saw the first broadcast of St Marie's choir from a new BBC Radio Station.

The following year it was discovered that the Church spire was in a dangerous condition owing to subsidence. The top third had to be taken down and rebuilt. This time it was topped by a new stainless steel cross.

During the 1920's a parish magazine was published monthly. Unfortunately, few copies survive, but they give a glimpse of parish life in those days. We read that in June 1922 Sr Mary Agnes SND retired from St Marie's School. Canon Dolan was glowing in his praise of her. She had been instrumental in starting the Guild of St Agnes for girls over school age as a preparation for entering the Children of Mary. At the time the Guild was the most flourishing in the parish. In 1923 the Redemptorists preached a mission in the parish. The priests were Frs Vassall-Phillips, Jackson and Ahearne. A feature was the large number of men who attended 9.30 Mass and instruction every morning.

In the January issue of 1926, the Canon mentions the reopening of St William's Church after a considerable enlargement. "St William's," he says, "may now truly be called a Church." On 18 January G.K. Chesterton came to Sheffield to address the Catholic Women's League. He gave an assessment of the flippancy of the thought of the day.

In March the news was that a new wireless set had been given to the girls' school at Sheaf Gardens, and the educational value of this new invention is loudly acclaimed.

In October the Canon wrote of the demand for a new Church School:

There is a strong emigration from the poorer parts of the city to the Manor Estate; and if there is no opposition I hope to put up a temporary school within the next few months. It will take the form of an army hut. The demand for a Church and School is most insistent. Last Sunday 120 or 130 people attended Mass in the temporary Council School; and I am going up there every Sunday. When my big scheme is finished it will be dedicated to St Theresa of the Infant Jesus, commonly known as the Little Flower. When I was in Rome last year for the Jubilee, the canonisation of the Little Flower took place in St Peter's and I took part in the ceremony.

Once the foundation stone of the new St Theresa's was laid there was hard work to be done in the parish to raise money to pay for it. The Canon donated a diamond ring he had been given, and a raffle was arranged which raised £64.0s.9d. This was considered to be a great success.

1929 was the centenary of Catholic Emancipation. There was to be a grand celebration in London, to which a small party from the parish was sent. They travelled in Canon Dolan's old Fiat car, which was nothing to look at but very dependable. The first event was a men's demonstration in the Albert Hall. Seven thousand were there to hear Cardinal Bourne, the main speaker, and the meeting ended with them all singing Credo III—a Dominican Friar keeping time with a billiard cue painted white.

Thousands also took part in a silent walk to Southwark Cathedral on the Sunday afternoon.

Eighty parishioners journeyed via Holyhead and Dun Laoghaire to Dublin for the Eucharistic Congress of June 1932. The weather was marvellous and an estimated one million men (for it was for men only) attended the final Pontifical High Mass in Phoenix Park.

An edition of the parish magazine of the 1930's gives us an idea of normal parish life. The Canon wrote:

> Though reports are seldom sent in, I know that good work is going on. Real work needs no advertising. St Anne's Guild, now affiliated to the nation-wide Union of Catholic Mothers meets every Monday and is at the moment busily preparing for their annual outing to the seaside. The Children of Mary holds its sewing meetings every Tuesday evening; its Sunday meeting each fortnight for Office and Devotions; and it has just had a week's Retreat. The Rosary Confraternity still flourishes under the spiritual direction of Fr Hewitt. He is also the inspiring leader of the Legion of Mary, which is doing excellent work for its members and for the parish. The Choir, especially the junior section, has been reinforced in numbers and refreshed in spirit by Fr Palfreyman. The Guild of St Stephen, too shy to send in a report, meets once a month. Recent topics for discussion have been Holy Week, and the Sacraments, Mass Vestments—their history and meaning, the prayers and Prefaces of the Missal. The APF [Association for the Propagation of the Faith] continues its apostolic endeavours, unnoticed and unsung. The Young Christian Workers, designated by Pope Pius XI authentic Catholic Action, has at last come out into the open, and has held a successful rally.

In fact, the Young Christian Workers began to get ambitious. In 1935, a group set off to cycle to Wigan to attend a Rally. Leaving on Good Friday, they returned safely on Easter Tuesday. Two years later, a saving club was established and preparations put in hand to attend the International Congress in Rome the next year. However, the Munich Crisis and the threat of war meant the Congress was cancelled. One of the group who was very keen to go did finally get to Rome; though he had to wait until 1944, travelling via North Africa and Southern Italy. He was then not with the YCW but with the British Army.

Meanwhile the growth of the Catholic population of the city continued. Father McNamara was put in charge of the new mission of St Theresa's in 1929, living for a while at St Marie's before moving to the estate. In 1934 Fr J. Grogan succeeded him and the following year the mission was made into a separate parish.

As the Wybourne estate grew, Mass was said on Sundays in the Chapel at City Road Cemetery, then in a room in the new council school. Land was bought for a new Church and school, which would be St Oswald's. Much later, when the Church was built, the parish was also dedicated to Our Lady, Queen of Heaven. In 1987 the parish returned to being known by its original designation, St Oswald's.

A feature of St Marie's until the 1930's was the reservation of places in the nave. The old benches had name plaques on them. The Duke of Norfolk had plaques on two benches reserved for members of his family. Some benches were equipped with a drawer that could be locked, where the owner would keep his missal or prayerbook. About once a quarter, a notice appeared on one of the Church pillars: "Bench rents now due".

During this decade the Passionists from Myddleton Lodge in Ilkley gave the annual Mission, and Ilkley became a popular place for choir trips and for the parish scout camp.

In 1935 a fault was discovered in the church spire which had to be demolished to half its size and once again rebuilt. This was the year of King George V and Queen Mary's jubilee. The steeple-jacks made a crown holding illuminations and this was placed on the top of the completed steeple. This same crown was re-erected on the steeple for the Silver Jubilee of Queen Elizabeth II, and made its third glittering appearance for the Centenary of Consecration year 1989.

Another great event for the Catholic Community of England was the canonisation in Rome of the two-best known English martyrs, Thomas More and John Fisher. Canon Dolan was determined to go. He fully entered into the celebrations and seemed to feel a life-time's dream had been fulfilled. However, the journey and the exertion proved too much. On his return he fell victim to pneumonia. He was taken into Claremont Nursing Home, then in Claremont Crescent, where he died very suddenly, just before Midnight on Wednesday 29 May 1935. His death was a great shock to the people of the parish and to the city as a whole. St Marie's lost an outstanding priest, the children a loving friend, the Catholic community a tenacious fighter for Catholic rights.

The day after his death the Morning Telegraph had the headline: "Canon Dolan Dead—Great Loss to Sheffield Catholic Circles". There followed a long article with a photograph. The following day an article under 'Current Topics' gave some interesting reflections on the Canon's character:

Curiously enough our first conversation with him, many years ago, was not exactly friendly. We had written something, the purport of which we have forgotten, but which apparently conveyed some reflection on his Church. He came through to us on the telephone and told us quite bluntly that what we had written was 'all wrong'. We gently replied that the facts were as stated. 'Yes', he said, 'it is not the facts I am questioning but the inference you draw from them.' We reminded him of this incident not very long ago but he had forgotten it. 'I like to remember the pleasant things in life', he remarked with his genial laugh.

The parish magazine also carried an obituary:

Our dearly-loved Canon has gone from us. Only the last issue of this magazine contained his Editorial in his best sparkling vein. We shall all of us miss him, though perhaps not all in the same way. For one, it will be his capacity for affection; for another, his charming hospitality, which had the art of making his house your own; for another, perhaps his hearty laughter and jolly humour, which could so brighten up public and parochial meetings.   Our dear old Canon never laid claim to intellectual profundity or subtlety; but all the same he had choice and rare talents . . . His motives were always transparent and his sincerity obvious. He simply went straight for what he wanted, and woe to you if you stood in his way! But even when he came down hard and heavy we still loved him—he was so impersonal an adversary that he still remained a friend—and nobody could bury a hatchet so irretrievably as he could.

The Bishop of Leeds, Bishop Cowgill, was himself ill and unable to celebrate the Requiem Mass. In his place stood the Vicar General, Monsignor Hawkswell. The panegyric was preached by Fr L. Gallon. The Church was packed with mourners from every parish and walk of life. The Lord Mayor and Lady Mayoress (Alderman and Mrs Turner), representatives from the Education Committee, the Provost of Sheffield, representatives from the Methodist Church and the Upper Chapel were present. The route to the cemetery was lined with people. Many thronged the cemetery itself, showing how much people from all over the city thought of him.

The Yorkshire Telegraph and Star on the Saturday evening gave a full account of the funeral the day before:

Hundreds of women wept as Fr Gallon delivered his oration on the life of Canon Dolan. 'How utterly impossible it is to give a resume of the life of your late Canon,' said Fr Gallon. 'His life was so full, the demands upon his resources so great and the noble characteristics of his intellect and will so beautiful and idealistic, that words fail miserably in portraying the personality of this great man.'

It was decided that a memorial window be erected in his memory. This was put in the old Baptistery, now the Reconciliation Rooms. It depicts three saints closely connected with the Canon's life—St Oswald, his patron, in the centre, flanked by St John Baptiste de la Salle, for the Canon established the De La Salle College, and St

Theresa of Lisieux, the patroness of the last parish he founded.

Canon Thomas Bentley

Canon Bentley was appointed to succeed Canon Dolan, but the pattern of forty years previous was to be repeated. Canon Bentley was unable to settle in Sheffield and after a year he was appointed to St Robert's, Harrogate. His replacement was a native of Sheffield, and of the parish—Fr James Bradley. He was to remain for fifteen years.

Canon James Bradley

9. Canon Bradley

James Bradley attended St Marie's School on Edmund Road (now demolished). As a teenager he expressed the desire to be a priest and was sent by the bishop to Douai Abbey in France to begin his studies. During his time there, the anti-clerical government in France drove out the monks, who came to England and settled near Reading. He moved to Ushaw where he completed his studies and was ordained in 1910. His first appointment was to St Bede's Grammar School in Bradford. Throughout his life he returned to Bradford to lecture in philosophy to the VIth formers of St Bede's and St Joseph's College for girls. During the First World War he served as a chaplain in the forces. After the war he was a curate in his home parish of St Marie's, with Canon Dolan as his Parish Priest. Eventually he was sent to be Parish Priest in the Sacred Heart parish in Ilkley, to return to St Marie's in succession to Canon Bentley.

On Easter Sunday 1939 the foundation stone was laid for a new school-chapel on the Wybourn Estate. The official opening took place on 25 April 1940. The school was named St Oswald's in memory of Canon Dolan.

In the blitz later in the year the oldest Catholic School in the city, St Marie's girls' school in Sheaf Gardens, was destroyed. The children had already been evacuated to Melton Mowbray in Leicestershire. Their departure date was 1 September—the day Hitler invaded Poland. There was a great deal of excitement among the children as they marched along Suffolk Road to the station. The teachers were with them and many parents came to say goodbye. The excitement increased as the train moved out, since for many of the children it was their first railway journey. On arrival at Melton Mowbray they were taken to a large hall. Here each child was given a carrier bag containing food for immediate consumption. Then the children were allocated families who were to take care of them, though twelve St Marie's children were placed at the Franciscan Convent. Two days later war was declared. Canon Bradley visited the children on several occasions, bringing ice-cream and sweets. Parents visited their children and some brought them home. As the immediate scare over air-raids decreased, most were brought back.

Sheffield was, however, a prime target for the bombers since, as in the first war, the silver and cutlery trade had given way to the manufacture of small arms, aircraft components and other war items. For nine hours on the night of December 12th/13th, and for three hours on the night of the 15th bombs fell. Industry largely escaped, but the commercial side of the city was badly hit, and eighty thousand homes were affected.

The school received the blast from a land-mine dropped on the Goods-Station. A member of staff, Miss Hazel Worth, came in the following day to rescue as many books and as much equipment as possible. Progress was slow but the labour was fruitful and much was saved and taken to the Parish Room at the Church for safe-keeping. However, when the staffroom was reached there was a different picture. Everything had disappeared—pots, pans, the gas-fire, even the sink. The room was completely bare. Then it was discovered that the piano from the infant department had also been taken. Recovery work ended when the police arrived to announce unexploded bombs in the area, forcing everyone to leave.

The girls and infants, now without a school, moved up to the boys' school on Edmund Road. They took over the ground floor, the boys using the upper floor. It thus became an all-age mixed school, which it remained until the implementation of the 1944 Education Act. The school suffered from many disadvantages, not least the fact that it had no air-raid shelters. The children were to use the shelters at Duchess Road School and this necessitated a weekly practice up and down the road in case of any day-time raids. None ever came, but the exercises no doubt proved great fun for the pupils and further hassle for the teachers.

For fear of the bombs, the main stained glass windows of the church were removed and stored for the duration of the war in part of the Nunnery Pit. The windows were boarded up. The congregation were rehearsed to leave the Church quickly and in good order in case of daylight raids. Canon Bradley, watch in hand in the pulpit, timed the congregation's exit.

After the war, a group of the Free Polish Army was demobbed in North Nottinghamshire. Many made their way to Sheffield with their chaplain, Fr Michael Szymankiewicz. He came to the central Church and asked for hospitality. Canon Bradley gave him a warm welcome, said he could stay as long as he liked, and said he must work to keep the Polish community together. From Easter 1948 to the present day, St Marie's has been the parish Church of the Polish people of Sheffield.

The post-war period was one of great expansion. The place of Catholic Schools had been protected and strengthened by the provisions of the 1944 Education Act. Vast amounts of money were raised, especially through football pools. It was a period of enthusiasm and revival. Mass rallies were held. In 1950 Fr Heenan of the Catholic

Missionary Society filled the City Hall. He was invited to return the following year, but by then he had been appointed Bishop of Leeds.

1950 was the centenary of St Marie's. The Church was decorated and the most famous preacher in the land, Monsignor Ronald Knox was invited to preach. Eight masses were celebrated to accommodate all the people before the great celebration of Pontifical High Mass at 11.15 on Sunday 3 September. Admission was by ticket only and every seat was taken. The Diocese of Leeds was vacant since the death of Bishop Poskitt the previous February. Bishop Brunner, auxiliary Bishop of Middlesbrough, came to offer the Mass. He was assisted by the Abbot of Douai Abbey and the Administrator of St Ann's Cathedral in Leeds, Monsignor John Dinn. The Lord Mayor and Lady Mayoress, Alderman and Mrs Keeble Hawson, together with the leader of the Council, Alderman J.H. Bingham, were among the guests. Most of the city clergy were there together with two sons of the parish—Fr Dignam S.J. Rector of Spinkhill and Fr (later Mgr) M. Sweeney, Headmaster of St Bede's, Bradford.

In his sermon Mgr Knox said:

> We can look back down three separate vistas of experience. This building typifies, in the first instance, the age-long permanence of the Catholic Church; all the more readily because, by happy accident, the year it was raised was the year in which the English hierarchy was restored. Or again, it records the continuous life of a single parish; a hundred years of patient witness to the Christian faith, here in the heart of a great city. Or finally, it may make us think of the multitudinous obscure lives that were lived in the shadow of this Church, and drew from it the sacramental strength that went with them on their journey. How many have been regenerated at that font; how many secrets, never repeated to human ears, have been whispered through the grills of those confessionals; what multitude have fed at those altar rails; how many of the faithful departed that bell has rung to their rest; all the unwritten stories that are commemorated in these stones.

On 12 March 1951 John Carmel Heenan was consecrated Bishop of Leeds. He was a man of great charm, a gifted speaker, and had fresh and enthusiastic ideas. He was convinced that the advantages in a priest staying many years in a parish were outweighed by the new opportunities and freshness that can come to both priest and people by a change. So he set about moving the clergy with a will. So thorough was he that the diocese became known as 'the Cruel See'. It was said that when the clergy met, their greeting was not 'How are you?' but 'Where are you?' St Marie's was much affected by this policy. Within a short time all the priests had been moved and a new team took over. Canon Bradley was transferred to St Ann's in Leeds to become the Cathedral Administrator, and the Administrator, Mgr John Dinn, came to St

Marie's. Mgr Dinn was the Vicar General so his arrival was seen as an upgrading of St Marie's to be the second most important Church in the Diocese.

Nevertheless, there was great sadness in the parish, not least on the part of Canon Bradley himself. He had been born and bred in the parish. He loved the place and the people. In his time of office he had ensured that the liturgy was carried out with great dignity. The Men's Choir sang the Solemn High Mass in Plain Chant every Sunday. He had seen St Theresa's established as a parish in its own right, and a school set up on the Wybourn.

Monsignor John Dinn

10. Mgr John Dinn

Among other innovations introduced by the new Bishop was the Perpetual Novena to our Lady of Perpetual Succour, the Principle Patroness of the Diocese, in every parish. A Redemptorist priest, Fr Deery, came to preach a triduum at St Marie's to establish the Novena here, which was held every Wednesday evening. Ordinations were no longer to be celebrated exclusively at the Cathedral. On 19 July 1953 Fr Brian Green and Fr Bernard Collins, both from St Patrick's parish were ordained at St Marie's. The first ordinations here since 1917.

Great changes were taking place in the universal Church. The encyclical letter of Pope Pius XII "Mystici Corporis" which emphasised the Church as priests and people together, underpinned the liturgical revival which was already taking place. The first changes concerned Holy Week whose celebration had become a clerical prerogative, the people merely visiting the Altar of Repose on Maundy Thursday, Stations on Good Friday and Confession on the Saturday in preparation for receiving Holy Communion on Easter Sunday. In theory the Easter Vigil was the climax of the Church's year. This was now to become a reality. By a decree of Pius XII the reformed Vigil was to be celebrated around Midnight. St Marie's, under the enthusiasm of one of the new priests, Fr Terence White, wholeheartedly adopted this celebration. Then came the development of the 'Dialogue Mass'. On Sundays one of the priests would be in the pulpit while another celebrated Mass, and he would lead the people in answering the Latin responses. The rules of fasting from midnight in preparation for receiving Holy Communion were relaxed to three hours, and so the times when Mass could be celebrated were broadened. Evening Mass became established, and the Sunday evening dialogue Mass with hymns became a crowded occasion at St Marie's. This led to the daily lunch-time Mass which is still so appreciated today. Great numbers of people were seeking admission to the Church in these years. The Legion of Mary took upon itself the task of organising 'Talks for non-Catholics'. In October 1952 one thousand two hundred invitations were sent out, following a house-to-house visitation.

In the 1950's the city was expanding westwards. A lot of private housing was being built in the Lodge Moor area. The Sisters of Notre Dame built a new Chapel in their convent grounds at Oakbrook. The foundation stone was laid in 1954. When the building was opened a public Mass was celebrated each Sunday morning. It was clear that a new parish should be formed in the area, and Mgr Dinn began looking for a suitable site for a Mass Centre. An opportunity arose when he was away on holiday in the United States. The old Church of England Schoolroom on Benty Lane at Crosspool came on the market. A difficulty arose over its sale to the Catholic community. Fr McGettigan who was in charge of the parish, gained the help of Mr Coates, a man prominent in Sheffield Market. He bought the property as a warehouse for his business and then sold it to the parish as a Chapel of Ease. The Notre Dame Sunday Mass was transferred to this little Chapel of St Francis.

The Chapel was furnished with the best of the benches from St Marie's, though all were getting somewhat worse for wear. New benches were acquired for St Marie's and new lighting and new decoration transformed the interior of the Church.

Mgr Dinn was a keen pilgrim. He led a large group of parishioners to Rome for the Marian Year celebrations of 1954. He promoted the annual Diocesan pilgrimage to Lourdes, and encouraged the Sheffield Council for Catholic Action to organise an annual pilgrimage to the national shrine of our Lady at Walsingham. This pilgrimage still takes place today.

On 2 May 1957 Bishop Heenan was appointed Archbishop of Liverpool and a few months later Dr George Patrick Dwyer succeeded him in Leeds. The new Bishop appointed a new Vicar General and Mgr Dinn was made Provost of the Leeds Diocesan Chapter.

Greater changes were taking place in the wider Church. In 1958 Pope Pius XII died. His successor, John XXIII, could hardly have been more in contrast to his predecessor. Pius was tall, thin and aristocratic; John was small, stout and clearly of peasant stock. It seemed the Cardinals had elected a caretaker Pope, who would soon make way for Pius' senior advisor, Giovanni Montini who had only recently been appointed Archbishop of Milan. How wrong everyone was.

These were years of school building in the city in line with the provisions of the 1944 Education Act. Before this, children who passed the eleven-plus exam went to one of the Grammar Schools—De La Salle or Notre Dame. The rest remained in the all-age Parish School until they were fourteen years old. These schools provided education in a family atmosphere. Teachers knew the families and the families knew the school. Bonds of loyalty were forged. The Act sought to give non-Grammar School pupils better facilities, which meant larger schools serving a wider catchment area. Many priests, while welcoming this, feared that in the changes they might lose sight of their parishioners if their schooling continued outside the parish. The Diocese decided that these new schools would be built on a deanery basis. St Peter's School was opened in the north of the City in 1959. Mgr Dinn acquired the farm land on Granville Road which was owned by the Duke of Norfolk and which had long been used by the Catholic Community as a rallying point for large gatherings, especially at Whitsun. The new School, to be dedicated to St Paul, was to open in Autumn 1962.

The Duke of Norfolk was invited to perform the official opening the following Summer. However the Duke was sent to represent the Queen at the funeral of Pope John XXIII, and at the coronation of his successor Paul VI. Hence, the opening ceremony was performed by Bishop Dwyer.

On 24 September 1962, Mgr Bradley died in retirement at Bristol. Mgr Dinn was determined that the parish should give its son who had served it as curate and parish priest the final honours. The body was brought back and the Requiem celebrated with a crowded congregation. James Bradley was buried in the priests' vault in the City Road Cemetery.

At the time Mgr Dinn was in perfect health; but one year to the day later, on 24 September 1963 he died in Claremont Nursing Home after a short illness. The Bishop returned from the Second Vatican Council for the Requiem. The streets were lined to the cemetery.

Mgr John Dinn had served the parish for fourteen years. He had done great work in the field of education, serving on the City Council's Education Committee. Despite having much diocesan work in his roles as Vicar-General and Provost, he was a devoted Parish Priest and a worthy leader of the Church in Sheffield.

Canon George Collins

11. Canon George Collins

In October 1964 George Collins, a native of Rotherham, was appointed Parish Priest. After his ordination he had served with Mgr Dinn at Leeds Cathedral before taking charge, at a very early age, of Holy Rosary Parish, Leeds. In 1951 he had moved to Sheffield at the same time as John Dinn, but to go to St Patrick's.

His time here was to be one of great changes. These began at his induction ceremony. Bishop Dwyer came from Rome full of ideas of the Council and insisted on celebrating the Induction Mass on an altar facing the people. A temporary altar was constructed and placed outside the Rood Screen and altar rails. Few people in the crowded Church were able to see anything since the altar was on the floor of the Church. Afterwards the altar was placed inside the Rood Screen, and the lectern was placed under one of the arches. This temporary arrangement lasted for seven years.

A top priority for the new parish priest was the replacement of St Marie's School at Edmund Rd which was ready to be condemned. After much searching the Canon persuaded the Sheffield Authorities to earmark a site on Granville Road for the new school.

Bishop Dwyer was appointed Archbishop of Birmingham in 1965. The following May Bishop Wheeler, who was auxiliary Bishop in Middlesbrough, came to Leeds. For many years there had been talk about the division of Leeds Diocese. The first step was taken when the new Bishop petitioned the Holy See for an auxiliary Bishop. He was granted one in December 1967. It was Gerald Moverley who would be resident in Sheffield. Accordingly, he was consecrated in St Marie's on 25 January 1968 in the most splendid ceremony the Church had seen and took over the pastoral care of the South of the Diocese.

The Consecration of Bishop Gerald Moverley

In the summer of that year Canon Collins moved to St Robert's, Harrogate. This became the opportunity for dividing the parish.

The fast-growing Lodge Moor area became the new parish of St Francis. Its first Parish Priest was Fr Ronnie Fox who returned to the Diocese after many years teaching at Ushaw College. The new Parish Priest of St Marie's was to be Father Stephen Sullivan who had served here as a curate to Mgr Dinn, and had recently opened the new parish at Brinsworth.

Monsignor Stephen Sullivan

12. Mgr Stephen Sullivan

By 1969 the changes in the liturgy had been implemented and it was clear the architectural design of the Sanctuary was wholly unsuitable. The emphasis was on participation but the Rood Screen set up a barrier between the priest and people. If the new liturgy was to succeed, changes were necessary. Mgr Sullivan grasped the nettle.

The first consultant produced a scheme that was far too expensive. The second, J.J. Frame of Cowfold in Sussex, had just completed the re-ordering of the Cathedral in Gibraltar. He had a clear vision of what was needed, and inspired confidence. Under his guidance the work began in 1970. Two years chaos followed. The Rood Screen was dismantled, the sanctuary was brought forward, the altar frontal was sunk into the reredos and a new altar erected, the Church was decorated, with the intricate carving and decoration being highlighted. During the period of renovation, the Provost of Sheffield Cathedral offered his Church for our daily Masses. This kindness was commemorated by a plaque donated and unveiled by the Lord Lieutenant, Mr Gerard Young, in that Cathedral. On Friday 9th September 1972, the restored Church was opened and the new altar was consecrated by Bishop Moverley.

The following month, through the generosity of the Department of the Environment and the City Fathers the outside of the Church was cleaned by sandblasting. The black grime which coated the Church for over a century gave way to the mellow stone original.

Canon Collins had engaged an architect to draw up plans for the new St Marie's School on the ear-marked site on Granville Road. However, by the time the school was on the building programme of the Local Education Authority, important changes had taken place. The Canon had moved and the other Catholic Schools in the area, St Oswald's and St Theresa's, had empty places. The situation had to be reviewed. There was no Catholic School provision near the new St Francis Parish in the West. A search was made in the Ecclesall Road area, but no site was available. The Sisters of Notre Dame showed willingness to allow a school to be built at the entrance of their convent grounds. Happily the original plans could be easily adapted to the new site. The change of plan came as a shock to parents and staff and a few stormy meetings took place. Time has proved the wisdom of the change. The new school was opened the same week as the reordered Church in September 1972 by the Secretary of the Catholic Education Council, Richard Cunningham.

The old School in Edmund Road was still a sound building and plans were discussed to keep it in use. The first idea was to give it a dual purpose: a youth club on the ground floor, and a Hostel for homeless men on the upper floor. The need for such a hostel was increasing as the numbers of tramps calling at St Marie's and the other city centre Churches gave witness. An ecumenical committee had been set up to look at ways of resolving this problem. However, once the plan was known, numerous objections were raised by the people of the area, claiming that such people would be a danger to the local children. The plan was shelved. Within a year vandals had set fire to the building and it had to be destroyed. The idea for a tramps hostel went ahead and a property was purchased in Hanover St. It was named 'Bethlehem House' and for the first few years it was staffed on a voluntary basis by parishioners of St Marie's. It was later taken over on a fully professional basis.

Another important social need was answered with the establishing of a branch of the Samaritans. The Reverend Chad Varah, the founder, had visited Sheffield a few years earlier and his visit bore fruit in a steering committee on which Mgr Sullivan represented the Catholic Church. After much careful preparation the service was set up in rooms in Carver Street Methodist Church. The Samaritans have gone from strength to strength, with members of the Catholic Community being greatly involved, such as the late Frank Woulfe, its Director for many years, and Jerry Fitzpatrick, for a long time its Secretary.

By the time the third deanery Secondary Modern School had been opened in 1965 under the patronage of St John Fisher at Beaver Hill, Handsworth, the majority of the County Schools in the city had become Comprehensive and the eleven-plus examination had been abolished. This left the Catholic Community with a dilemma: either it had to continue with selection to Grammar Schools through an eleven-plus exam of its own, or plans had to be laid to go comprehensive. Many meetings, discussions and arguments took place and eventually a compromise plan was reached. The Catholic system would go entirely comprehensive. The three secondary modern schools would become mixed middle schools and the two grammar schools would be single sex upper schools. The Sisters of Notre Dame were a little reluctant; the De

La Salle Brothers seemed enthusiastic. However, before the plan could be put to the Secretary of State for Education and Science, the consent of the Provincials of the religious orders was required. When formally asked, the Sisters of Notre Dame readily agreed, but the Brothers declined on the grounds that they could not promise either the personnel or the capital that the plan required. This came as a great blow to the Bishop. The eleven-plus had already ceased and a scheme of 'guided parental choice' was quickly introduced while a new plan was put together. Since the Brothers could not promise to be full partners in the reorganisation, it was decided that the College should amalgamate with St Paul's as an 11-18 mixed Comprehensive School to be called 'All Saints', operating at first on the two sites, though eventually the Brothers sold the Scott Road premises and the entire school was housed on the Granville Road Site using many temporary terrapin classrooms.

Notre Dame would also be a mixed 11-18 Comprehensive School, also on two sites, at Cavendish Street and Oakbrook. The other two Secondary Modern Schools, St Peter's and St John Fisher, would become 11-16 Comprehensive Schools. This plan, it was felt, best used the buildings that already existed and was the least expensive. What was not fully appreciated was the massive fall in school rolls that was to take place. By the time the Comprehensive system was fully in operation there were many more places in Catholic schools than there were children for them. The 11-18 schools were more popular than the 11-16 whose very viability was thus threatened. The Catholic system was caught in an invidious position: the smaller schools had empty places and so the bigger schools were unable to attract grant-aid from the Department of Education and Science to provide adequate permanent accommodation for those on roll. The temporary accommodation at All Saints was deteriorating; the Cavendish Street building was decaying; but parental choice was firm in supporting these two schools in preference to the more modern provision in the 11-16 schools. A traumatic period of negotiation followed, which led to the closure first of St John Fisher's (1981), and then St Peter's (1985). This meant that the Diocese was in a stronger position to seek grant-aid from the D.E.S. for permanent building at the remaining schools. After much discussion, the diocesan case was in large measure conceded by the Department. The Cavendish Street site closed in 1988 after one hundred and twenty-seven years, and the school was housed on one site at Oakbrook on the Fulwood Rd, with the building of a Sports Hall, a laboratory block, extensive internal renovations and the acquisition of the Convent from the Notre Dame sisters as a teaching block. The sisters moved house for the fourth time and took up residence in Ashdell Rd.

Meanwhile the first moves were made at All Saints to move out of the temporary accommodation after twelve years. The first phase of a three part building programme got under way in 1988. After many years in the doldrums, amid bitterness and recrimination, Catholic secondary schools are well-established and are able to rejoice in having two of the best comprehensive school sites in the city from which they will proclaim the Christian message.

By 1968 the renewal engendered by the Second Vatican Council was filtering down to diocesan and parish level. Fr Donal O'Leary was appointed to the staff of St Marie's to establish a Catechetical Centre in Sheffield. He began his task with characteristic enthusiasm. A major difficulty he encountered was lack of space. The only available rooms were the choir room, which was small and not in the best of condition, and a room under the large sacristy which had once been a youth club, and had become something of a dumping ground. These two rooms were completely renovated. The choir room became a library and resource centre, the lower room a meeting room. With the R.E. Centre thus established, the great task of bringing the Vatican Council to the people began. Many distinguished speakers came to the centre, and much good work was done. Fr O'Leary left to take up a teaching post at St Mary's Twickenham, and Fr Brendan McKeefry came to continue the work.

The pressure on space was increasing. The Parish Room was wholly inadequate for the needs of the parish. When the leases on property on Norfolk Row came to an end, expansion became possible. Around that time a legacy was received from Mrs Beatrice Houlden and this helped finance the building of a parish hall within an office development project. The Hall on the first floor of the new building is known as The Houlden Hall in honour of the benefactor.

As the 1970's advanced, so the idea of a new diocese gained ground. On 30 May 1980 the Bull creating the new Diocese of Hallam was promulgated in Rome. The news only reached Sheffield in mid-June. The first Bishop of Hallam was Gerald Moverley and he decided that he would be enthroned on 3 July, the feast of Thomas the Apostle. There was little time for all to be prepared, but the preparations for the recently-formed diocese of East Anglia served well as a guide.

In a majestic ceremony the Bishop was enthroned by the Metropolitan—Archbishop Worlock of Liverpool, and Bishop Wheeler of Leeds. Many other bishops attended including Archbishop Dwyer of Birmingham, a former Bishop of Leeds. The Anglican Bishop of Sheffield, the President of the Free Church Council, the Lord Lieutenant of the County, Gerard Young who has attended Mass at St Marie's for more than fifty years, and the Lord Mayor of Sheffield all gave addresses of welcome in the course of the ceremony.

The new diocese was created from the dioceses of Leeds and Nottingham, the first time in England that there had been such a fusion. The name of the diocese came from the Anglo-Saxon name of the area. At the banquet in the Cutlers' Hall following the ceremony the Bishop of Nottingham wished the new diocese well and expressed deep regret at losing some of his priests and parishes.

Many expressed doubts as to the viability of such a small diocese, but nearly ten years later, the benefits of a compact diocese where Bishop, priests and people are well-known to each other have been abundantly proved.

When the new diocese was formed, St Marie's became a Cathedral. It was ready—made for the honour and well worthy of the title.

12. Fr John Ryan

Mgr Sullivan went into hospital after Easter of 1985 to have a hip-replacement operation. In his absence Fr John Ryan took over the day to day running of St Marie's. The following Autumn he was appointed Administrator and Mgr Sullivan moved to the formidable parish of the Annunciation, Chesterfield. (The well-worn path from St Marie's to St Robert's, Harrogate trodden by previous Rectors being no longer available with the creation of the new diocese.) Fr Ryan had been ordained in St Ann's Cathedral in Leeds after training at the Ven. English College, Rome. He served in St Peter-in-Chains, Doncaster before moving to St Marie's in 1983 to assist Mgr Sullivan both in the parish and in the work of the Schools' Commission.

In 1988 important restoration work was undertaken. A damp-course was put in round the outside walls and in the pillars.

This gave the opportunity to examine the old panelling which had been covered up in the re-ordering of 1971. This was removed, put through a sanding machine and replaced. For many years the Baptistery had been unused—a movable font being brought in to the Sanctuary for most baptisms. The font was brought from the Baptistery and placed in the North Transept. The floor of the Baptistery was lowered and new Reconciliation Rooms were built there. Finally the Church was decorated in preparation for the Centenary of Consecration celebrations.

A GUIDE TO
ST MARIE'S CATHEDRAL

– · –

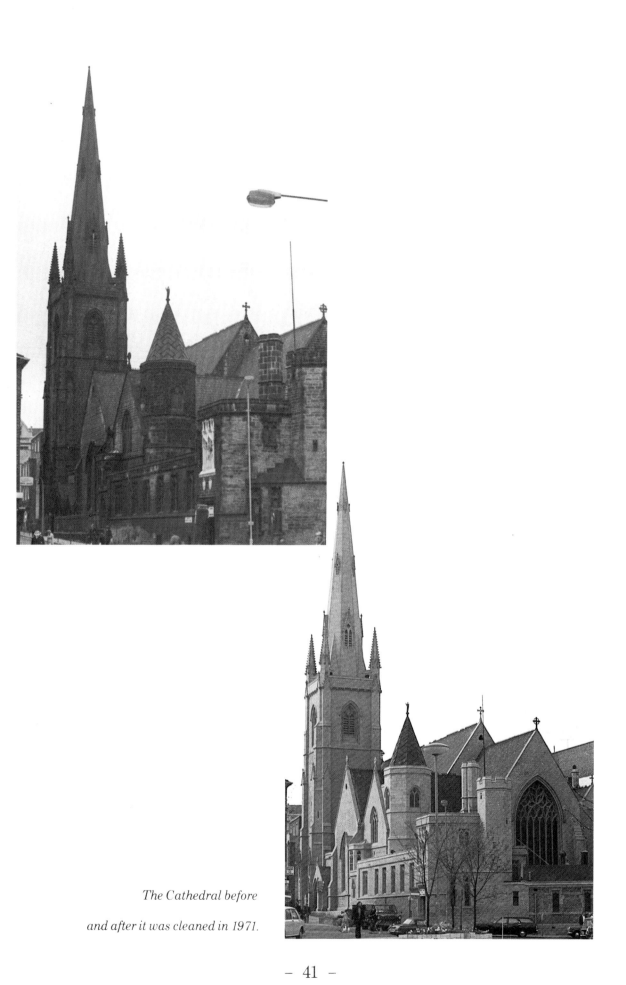

*The Cathedral before
and after it was cleaned in 1971.*

The Sanctuary, Bishop's Throne, and East Window.

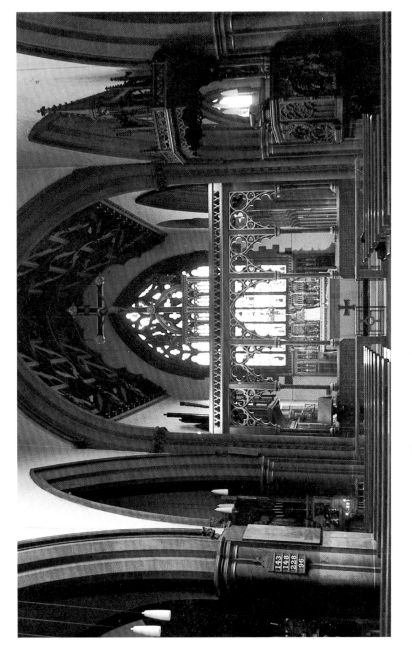

The Sanctuary before it was re-ordered in 1971.

The Sanctuary   after it was re-ordered in 1971.

The Bishop's Throne.

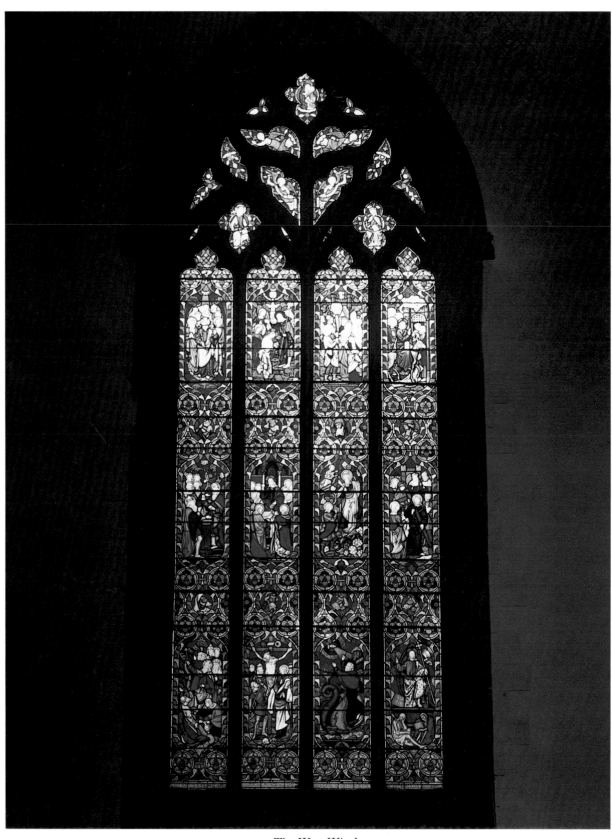

The West Window.

Jesus blessing the children.

Three canonised English martyrs: Thomas More, John Fisher, and Philip Howard.

Our Lady and St Henry.

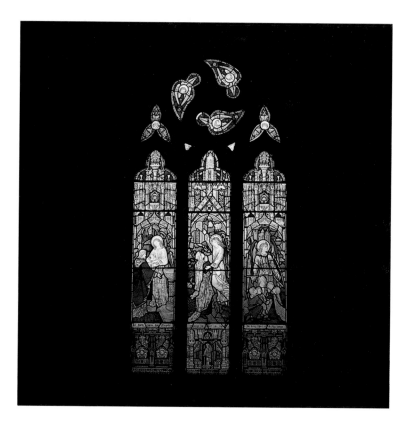

The Guardian Angel.

St Elizabeth of Hungary and St Mary Magdalene.

St Michael the Archangel tramples the Devil underfoot.

St Elizabeth and her small son John the Baptist.

St Michael the Archangel, St Thomas of Villanova,
St Mary Magdalene and St Elizabeth of Hungary.

The East Window.

Christ holding Host and Chalice whilst the Sun and Moon do him homage.

St Teresa of Avila, St Anne, St Joachim, and St Joseph.

Our Lady Queen of Hallam, with the Padley Martyrs: Nicholas Garlick
and Robert   Ludlum.

The Annunciation.

*St William of York with the symbols of the priesthood: chalice,
keys, Book of the Gospels, and ampula of holy oil.*

Our Lady Queen of Sorrows, St Teresa, and St Helen.

St Edward, King and Confessor, and St Hilda, Abbess of Whitby.

The Baptism of Our Lord, with St Simon and St Jude.

St John Baptiste De La Salle, St Theresa of Lisieux, and St Oswald, King and Martyr.

A GUIDE TO ST MARIE'S

As you enter St Marie's go first to the centre aisle and sit and pause for a moment. From here you can take in the single style and completeness of the interior. The eye is drawn to the great East Window overlooking the High Altar. The dominant colour of this window and, looking around, others in the side aisles is blue—the colour traditionally associated with Mary the mother of Christ, St Marie.

The gold colour present in the stonework indicates the sacred nature of this interior dedicated for prayer and the public worship of God.

Finally, before beginning a tour of the rich detail and symbolism to be found in St Marie's, notice how the eye tends to wander upward to the intricate design of the roof above the sanctuary. The pointed arches direct our thoughts heavenward.

Go now down the centre aisle but only about half way. Turn around to see . . .

THE WEST WINDOW

Stained-glass windows are not only objects of beauty and aids to prayer, but at their best are also teaching aids. The great West Window is all these things. The lights contrast Old and New Testament events, seeing the former as a type or prefiguration of the latter. If they are read across rather than down, then they follow the sequence of Our Lord's life. So the top of the first light on the left shows the crossing of the Red Sea, and next to it is Jesus' Baptism in the Jordan. Moving to the right there is David's triumphal entry into Jerusalem bringing the Ark of the Covenant, which prefigures Jesus' entry into Jerusalem as his Passion approached. Beneath these, again reading from the left, there is the offering of bread and wine by Melchisedech, the mysterious priest and king figure, who blessed Abraham and gave him bread and wine, foreshadowing Jesus' action at the Last Supper. Isaac carries the wood for Abraham's sacrifice in the third light which parallels Jesus' carrying his cross to Calvary. In the third row, Moses strikes the rock and water flows out, which is contrasted with the soldier piercing the side of Christ as he hangs on the cross, when blood and water flows out. Finally, Jonah emerges from the belly of the great sea-monster which foreshadowed Christ's Resurrection from the tomb.

At the apex the Virgin and Child are depicted. The tracery contains flowers and angels with scrolls. At the head of each pair of long lights is a quatrefoil. The left one contains the figure of Peace, bearing symbols of peace and plenty—the sceptre and bread and wine; on the right is the seated figure of Justice, blindfolded with a whip in one hand and the tablets of the law in the other. The heads between the pictures are various patriarchs and prophets.

The window was donated for the opening of the church in 1850, by Lady Augusta Mary Catherine Minna, Countess of Arundel and Surrey and mother of the Duke of Norfolk. It was commissioned from Messrs Hardman & Co. to a design by Augustus Welby Pugin.

Go now to the corner where you entered . . .

THE NORTH-WEST CORNER

Here is a window donated by Mr & Mrs John Barnascone which shows Jesus blessing children. The Sacred Heart, representing the love of Christ, is embellished in the apex. The rose of Yorkshire can be found just above the central columns. It is thought that the window was erected in memory of Canon Samuel Walshaw, Rector of St Marie's between 1866 and 1896 who was remembered for his devoted work in establishing Catholic schools in the City. There is a plaque on the window sill on the North Wall in his memory.

Notice in this corner of the Cathedral displays showing the life and concerns of the parish community. The Church is to be admired as a fine building but it is also the home of a living community of faith.

THE NORTH AISLE

The first window on the North wall portrays three of the canonised English Martyrs: Thomas More and John Fisher who were both beheaded on a charge of High Treason after refusing to take Henry VIII's Oath of Supremacy, and Philip Howard.

A bloodstained axe is shown at the feet of both Thomas and John. The purse with the initials 'HR' held by Thomas represents his position as Lord Chancellor of England. John Fisher, dressed as Bishop of Rochester, holds a book representing his many writings. He was created a Cardinal before his execution, but the Red Hat, seen in the depiction, was not allowed to be brought into England.

St Philip was a favourite of Elizabeth I until he became a Catholic in September 1584. Trying to escape to France, he was captured and imprisoned in the Tower of London. In 1589 he was condemned to death on the charge of having had a Mass said for the success of the Spanish Armada. He was not to be executed in public however, but was poisoned by the prison cook. Throughout his period of imprisonment, he devoted himself to spiritual exercises and writing religious verse.

Above each of the saints is his coat of arms. St Philip was the Earl of Arundel and eldest son of the fourth Duke of Norfolk. All three coats of arms are reproduced on the Roof of the Nave.

Above the North Door is a statue of the Virgin and Child which is believed to have come from the Chapel which stood here before the present Church was built. In the windows on either side are depicted Our Lady and St Henry. These windows were presented by Henry T. Bulmer, the artist who carried out much of the original decoration of the church, in memory of his mother, Sarah.

Next is the Guardian Angel Window whose colours are somewhat faded.

The statue of St Joseph was presented by Doctor Allanson in 1860 in memory of his wife who died in 1858, aged 25.

THE MORTUARY CHAPEL

Two decorated arches form the entrance to the Mortuary Chapel. The central pillar has the heavenly choir of angels sculptured around its capital.

A carved wood figure of St Cornelius stood under an oak canopy on the left hand pillar until it was stolen. The carving came from Belgium and had been presented in memory of Henry and Mary Beauvoisin.

By the Icon of Our Lady of Perpetual Succour there is a double light window portraying St Elizabeth of Hungary with flowers in her lap, and St Mary Magdalene holding a vase of precious ointment, with which she anointed the feet of our Lord in the house of Simon, the Pharisee. The window was donated in 1850 by Elizabeth Wake and Mary Ellison.

The Icon is a copy of the famous picture in the Church of St Alphonsus in Rome, which an ancient, though inauthentic, tradition held to be the work of the evangelist St Luke. Angels appear to the Child showing him the implements of his crucifixion. The Child starts in horror, and his sandal falls off. The Icon was presented by Miss Baillie of York in 1875. Seldom are there no candles burning before it. Our Lady of Perpetual Succour was named Patroness of the Diocese of Hallam when it was established in 1980.

The two single lights in the Chapel depict the triumph of good over evil. St Michael the Archangel tramples the devil underfoot; and St Elizabeth with her small son John the Baptist who pointed out Jesus as the Lamb of God who would take away the sin of the world.

The panel on the wall below these windows asks for prayers for the deceased clergy who have worked in the parish. Some of them are listed with the date of their anniversary. This was set up by Canon Walshaw but has not been kept up to date.

Above the altar is a fine wooden dossal, carved by Herr Petz of Munich. The centrepiece shows Christ's deposition from the cross. The side panels have rows of foliage and the first line of Psalm 129: 'Out of the depths . . .' This was presented by the Reverend D. Haigh of Erdington in memory of his friend Edward Bruce.

Beneath the altar is the effigy of Fr Charles Pratt, the Founder of St Marie's. It was sculpted by Thomas Earp, carver to the firm of George Myers, who built the Church and was said to be a good likeness. An angel kneels at his head, and his beloved little dog at his feet. In his hands he holds the Church he founded but never saw completed. The spire is shown unfinished. Originally the tomb was placed under an iron canopy between the Sanctuary and the Blessed Sacrament Chapel.

Names of deceased parishioners are visible on the tiled floor. The inscriptions ask for prayers for them. An 'Ave' (Hail Mary) and 'Pater' (Our father) are suggested.

On the wall are four wooden carvings showing the final stages of Christ's agony and death. These are the last four of a series of fourteen stations which begin on the opposite South wall. They are intended to aid prayer and reflection. The custom of having stations around the Church was brought by pilgrims returning from the Holy Land in the fourteenth century.

THE NORTH TRANSEPT

The Baptismal font was moved to its present position in 1988, linking the celebration of Baptism more closely to the celebration of the Eucharist. The eight sides are sunk in square sculptured panels, representing the seven sacraments and the crucifixion. Reading round the font find Baptism, Reconciliation, Holy Communion, Marriage, Confirmation, Anointing of the sick, Ordination.

The window here is by John Pearson. The four panels show St Michael the Archangel, St Thomas of Villanova, St Mary Magdalene, and St Elizabeth of Hungary. The Latin inscription below it reads:

> Pray for the soul of Michael Ellison, for many years most faithful steward of the most noble lords Bernard Edward, Charles Henry, Henry Granville Howard, Dukes of Norfolk, Lords of this Manor of Hallamshire. Strengthened by the last rites of the Church, he died on the thirteenth day of March 1861, aged 74. [Say an] Our Father and a Hail Mary.

At the top of the window is the Latin word Deus (God) and linked in the tracery the initial letters of the three Persons of the Trinity—'P' (Pater—Father), 'F' (Filius—Son) and 'SS' (Spiritus Sanctus—Holy Spirit).

The alabaster Pieta below the window to the right was sculpted by Frank Tory from a design by Charles Hadfield. The figure of Our Lady was after a cast sent to M.E. Hadfield by his friend A.W.N. Pugin. It was erected in memory of the architect of the Church by his family in March 1887. He had died two years earlier on March 9th at 72 years of age. He is buried in St Michael's Cemetery at Rivelin.

Beside this there is an alabaster and Hopton Wood tablet given by Charles and Emily Hadfield, the parents of two children who died very young in 1874 and 1875.

The statue of the Madonna and Child was carved in limewood by Herr Petz of Munich. This was another gift of Mary and Henry Beauvoisin. Both figures wear gilded, jewelled crowns which were donated by Matthew Ellison Hadfield. The shrine was erected in 1874. Its base is of alabaster, relieved with carved lilies and a gilded background, standing on a raised dais of fossil marble and encaustic tiles decorated with our Lady's emblem—the fleur de lys. The four illustrated panels of carved wainscot oak at the back of the statue are, from left to right, St Winefride, St John the Evangelist, St Dominic, and St Catherine of Alexandria, the Patroness of Sheffield. The canopy which tops the shrine is 22 feet (6.7m) above the floor. This shrine and the nearby Sacred Heart Shrine, have tables of six inch thick Derbyshire fossil marble slab, supported by twin columns of Frosterly fossil marble, originally in the Chapel of the nine altars of Durham Cathedral.

The panels on each side of the Sacred Heart statue (1877) show angels with censers. Below these are paintings by N.H.J. Westlake of Blessed Margaret Mary Alacoque and St Jane Frances de Chantal copied from authentic portraits. These are saints of the eighteenth century closely associated with the growth of devotion to the Sacred Heart. The shrine was designed by Charles Hadfield, and the statue is by Boulton.

Behind the Shrine is an opening leading to a flight of stone steps which, before 1972, led to the top of the Rood Screen which spanned the Chancel arch.

THE BLESSED SACRAMENT CHAPEL

Over the iron screen leading to the Blessed Sacrament Chapel hangs a burning lamp surrounded by six candles. The lamp is lit to show the Blessed Sacrament is present in the Tabernacle on the altar. This Chapel is a special place of quiet and private prayer. The lamp was given by Charles Hadfield, son of the architect of the Church and author of the History of the St Marie's Mission published in 1889. It was renovated in 1951 by Mr Edward Hirst, long-time Church Organist, in memory of his parents. It was placed in its present position in 1981 having previously been over the High Altar.

The screen, surmounted by seven candlesticks, contains emblems associated with the Blessed Sacrament and its institution by Christ at the Last Supper—the chalice, the lamb, the initials 'IHS' (the Greek letters JES meaning Jesus). These emblems together with grapes and wheat ears are also found in the bosses in the roof of the chapel.

Originally the windows were stained glass depicting St Charles and St Anastasia; and St Catherine of Alexandria and St Edmund of Canterbury. However, during the blitz of December 1940 an incendiary bomb set fire to sugar in the adjacent Tuckwood's Bakery, and the windows were destroyed in the heat, leaving only the tiny lights at the top of the windows. The windows remained opaque glass until a donation in 1988 by Neil Nicholson in memory of his wife Gillian, and by Gillian's mother, Margaret Dalton, in memory of her husband, allowed new windows to be put in, showing Jesus' baptism, and the descent of the Holy Spirit, thus bringing together the Sacrements of Initiation.

The three panelled window in the east wall was a gift of Mary Smelter, Mary Cadman and Sarah Ellison. The tracery shows three angels bearing scrolls with the word "Sanctus", and two holding crowns. Beneath are winged cherubim and the angelic host. The central light shows Christ holding host and chalice, while the Sun and Moon do him homage. Below the institution of the Last Supper is depicted. Woven throughout are vine leaves and grapes recalling the wine used in the Mass and Christ's description of himself as 'the True Vine'.

The reredos, designed by Hadfield, shows three seated angels, each holding a rounded shield which display: a pelican, which was taken as a symbol of the Eucharist from the mythical story that if the pelican could not find food, she would peck at her own breast to feed her young; the Paschal Lamb; and three ears of wheat.

The carving of the Last Supper on the North wall was donated by Mrs Teresa Ware in memory of her husband, Joseph.

THE SANCTUARY

Moving now to the centre of the Nave you are standing before the Sanctuary, the setting for the great ceremonies of the Cathedral. Overlooking all is the East Window. Totalling one thousand panes this window depicts events in the life of Our Blessed Lady: Reading the lights downwards from left to right—

Our Lady's Birth;

Her Presentation in the Temple;

Mary with her mother St Anne;

Mary's betrothal to Joseph;

The Annunciation;

Mary's Visitation to Elizabeth

The Nativity of our Lord;

The Adoration of the Magi;

The Presentation of Jesus in the Temple;

On the right of the centre panel:

The flight into Egypt;

The finding of the child Jesus in the Temple;

Jesus, carrying his Cross, meets his mother;

The Crucifixion with Mary at the foot of the Cross;

The Deposition;

A Resurrection appearance;

The Ascension;

The Descent of the Holy Spirit;

Our Lady's Dormition.

The centre panel depicts John's vision in the Book of revelation: The Lady, clothed with the Sun, with the moon at her feet, crowned with a halo of twelve stars. At her feet are the donors, Matthew and Sarah Hadfield. At the window's apex are the Trinity; beneath them is Mary seated; below her are her parents, St Joachim and St Anne, and our first parents, Adam and Eve; surrounding them are angels and various types of saints—abbesses, virgins, queens, popes, kings. In the inner elongated trefoil one angel is proclaiming, 'Mary is Queen' and the other holds a crown. The sun, moon and stars fill the interstices.

The window was designed by George Goldie, who became Hadfield's partner in 1850, and made by Wailes.

Below the window is a reredos designed by Pugin and carved by the Belgian sculptor Theodore Phyffers. In the four sunk panels are eight angels bearing instruments and emblems of the Passion—the Cross, the Crown of Thorns, nails and a hammer, pincers, a ladder, a spear, the garments stripped from Jesus for which lots were cast, the depiction of the Five Wounds of Christ, whips and a whipping-post.

About two feet forward of this is a second reredos where the original High Altar was positioned. Four panels represent the Cardinal Virtues: Prudence exemplified by Mary and Joseph's Betrothal; Justice by the Annunciation; Fortitude by Jesus' Carrying his Cross and meeting his Mother; and Temperance by the Holy Family in their home in Nazareth.

The original High Altar was dismantled after the First World War to be replaced, at the behest of Canon Dolan, by one in memory of the sixty-seven Sheffield men who died in the war. This second altar was of stone, carved and decorated in the 15th Century tradition of English illuminated work. It was consecrated by Bishop Cowgill on 29 June 1921, and dedicated on 1 July by Bishop Keatings, senior Catholic Chaplain to the Forces, in honour of the City Battalion who died at the Somme. This altar was removed in 1972, and a new altar introduced into the Sanctuary re-ordered for the New Rite of Mass. (Those who died in the Great War are still remembered on a memorial plaque on the right of the entrance to the old Baptistry, now the Reconciliation Rooms). The new altar, also of stone, was designed by J.J. Frame, carved and gilded in a style similar to the Memorial Altar. This altar was consecrated on 8 September 1972 by Bishop Moverley and Bishop Wheeler. The relics of both previous altars were cemented into the new.

When St Marie's became a Cathedral in 1980 the Bishop's Cathedra or Throne was introduced in front of the Reredos. The Throne itself was part of the old Choir Stalls, with carvings of Mary and the Angel Gabriel. It was seriously damaged by fire in a vandal attack in 1987.

Though the damage was extensive, the Throne was most skillfully and painstakingly restored by Fred Collier. The backing was made and painted by J. Lee. The Throne now stands in front of the old Tabernacle which was designed by Pugin.

On the Chancel Wall leading to the Blessed Sacrament Chapel is a plaque honouring the Church's Founder, Charles Pratt whose remains are under this spot. A brass memorial on the same wall commemorates the priests who served in the Sheffield Mission prior to St Marie's being built: Richard Rimmer, Michael Bimson, Thomas Fisher and Thomas Holden.

The Organ, a Thomas Lewis Tracker Organ, in a case of carved Austrian Oak carved by James Erskine Knox to a design of John Bentley, was donated by the 14th Duke of Norfolk in 1875. It contains 1,700 pipes. In 1986 the sound-boards were completely rebuilt by the Dronfield firm, Chalmers & Hyde. When new, the Organ cost £1,095; today its value is estimated between £180-200,000.

The Rood, the cross with the Mother of Jesus and the Beloved Disciple standing below, which is suspended from the ceiling was previously mounted on a Screen which ran right across the Chancel archway. This was removed in the 1972 renovations. The four evangelists are represented in their traditional symbols—Eagle (John), Lion (Mark), Bull (Luke), Man (Matthew).

The Sanctuary ceiling with its angels and stars is designed to raise the mind to thoughts of Heaven. It also represents the hosts of heaven overseeing the sacred ceremonies performed below.

THE NORFOLK CHAPEL

This is found to the right of the sanctuary. To the right of the Chantry Screen at the entrance to the Chapel is an alabaster statue of an angel given by Mrs Barnascone in memory of her husband John who died in 1930. Over the Archway are the family crests of Mr Frame and Mgr Sullivan, jointly responsible for the 1972 renovations. The tiled floor bears the initials of the Norfolk family, surmounted by a ducal coronet, and the initials of 'the Earl of Arundel and Surrey' with the Lion of the House and the motto 'Sola Virtus Invicta'. On the stone screen separating the Chapel from the Sanctuary is a request in Latin for prayers for the House of Norfolk.

Beneath the Screen are tiles in memory of the Sisters of Notre Dame, and there are also requests for prayers for Mary Smelter, who donated the Altar dedicated to St Joseph. Above the Altar is carved the death of St Joseph.

Opposite the Sanctuary Screen are panels of six Virgin Saints: Catherine, Barbara, Dorothy, Agnes, Clare and Margaret, together with alabaster statues of St Rose of Lima, St Margaret, and St Hilda of Whitby. This latter is carved from a piece of alabaster from Blyth Abbey, Nottinghamshire. Opposite is a statue of St Winefride.

THE SOUTH TRANSEPT

The painting on the right as one leaves the Norfolk Chapel is also of St Winefride, by Westlake. To the left by the door to the Cloister is a statue of St Theresa, given by Miss Keats in Canon Dolan's time. Over the door are escutcheons of Fr Pratt and Dr Briggs, Vicar Apostolic of the Northern District in 1847. The statue of St Patrick has a base of Connemara marble. It serves to recall the great Irish immigration following the potato famine of the 1840's.

The window on the South Wall, by William Wailes of Newcastle, depicts Sts Teresa of Avila, Anne, Joachim, and Joseph. The donor, Teresa Wright of Revell Grange is seen kneeling at her Patroness' feet. At the top of this window the tracery and design form a tiny rose window.

On the west wall of the Transept is a window depicting Our Lady Queen of Hallam, with the Padley Martyrs, Nicholas Garlick and Robert Ludlum, bearing the palms of martyrdom. These priests were arrested at Padley near Grindleford and were executed at Derby in July 1588. The Coats of Arms are those of Pope John Paul II and Bishop Moverley. The window was installed in 1980 to mark the creation of the new Diocese of Hallam. It is the work of Patrick Reyntiens, well-known for his work in Coventry Cathedral and Liverpool's Roman Catholic Cathedral.

THE MUNSTER (LADY) CHAPEL

The staircase to the right of the Cloister door leads to the Lady Chapel, which was donated by Henry Munster, as the floor of the Chapel testifies. The window on the right of the staircase, which dates from 1884, depicts the Annunciation, in memory of Carolina Bernasconi who died in 1879, aged 16; and St Joseph in memory of Charles and Constance Rimondi. It was designed by J.F. Bentley and made by Lavers, Barraud and Westlake. The altar is built up of solid slabs of polished Sicilian marble. The white marble statue of Our Lady of Mercy was sculptured in Rome. The crown is studded with crystals. The arcade above is supported by monoliths of green marble from the Pyrenees, with delicately sculptured capitals and bases of Hopton Wood stone. The lantern portion of the Oratory has three stained glass windows by Hardman: the centre illustrates the Coronation of Our Lady, and the sides angelic musicians.

On the right hand wall is a copy of the Icon of Our Lady of Czestochowa, Queen of Poland, the work of the Polish artist Stanislaw Frenkel. It was purchased by the Polish Community in Sheffield who settled here after the Second World War and made St Marie's their Parish Church, and this Chapel especially theirs. Below the Icon is a memorial to the Polish troops who died in that war.

THE SOUTH AISLE

The first of the Windows in the South Aisle depicts St William of York, with symbols of the priesthood—chalice, keys, Book of the Gospels, ampulla of holy oil. The window commemorates Fr William Parsons who was appointed Rector of the Sheffield Mission after the death of Fr Pratt.

The next window, which is by Hardman, pictures Our Lady of Sorrows, St Teresa and St Helen. Notice the representations of items associated with the death of Jesus and the sword of sorrow that Simeon, when the baby Jesus was presented at the Temple, prophesied would pierce her heart. The fifteen flowers in the design signify the rosary. The third, St Edward, King and Confessor and St Hilda, Abbess of Whitby.

The narrow door by the new Reconciliation rooms leads up to the Belfry. It seems a bronze bell was hung in the steeple when the Church was built, and to this were added eight steel bells erected by Naylor Vickers & Co. in July 1861. Canon Fisher offered the original bell to Naylor Vickers in part payment but strong representations from several members of the congregation prevented the transaction. These steel bells were not a success. They were removed to Birmingham and a peal of eight bronze bells (total 6 tons) were added to the Angelus bell (22 cwt.) in 1874, half the cost being met by the Duke of Norfolk, half by the congregation. They were reconditioned in 1934 and rehung the following year by Mears and Stainbank, of London, the original makers. The bells are regularly rung by the University Guild of Bell Ringers. The practice of ringing the Angelus Bell was instituted by Canon Walshaw in 1866 and continued up to the 1939-45 war. Mgr Dinn recommenced the custom; and an automatic mechanism was fitted in his memory as the memorial plaque testifies.

The picture of St Jude by the Belfry door was given by Mrs Gorka in memory of her husband.

Above the new Reconciliation Rooms are visible stained glass windows. In the South Wall the Baptism of Our Lord recalls that this was the Baptistery until 1988. St Simon is on one side and St Jude on the other. The window commemorates the Golden Wedding anniversary of John and Lavinia Barnasconie which fell on the feast day of these two saints.

The window in the West Wall commemorates Canon Oswald Dolan. The wall of the tower was cut through to house the window so it was formidable undertaking bringing welcome new light into the Baptistery. The left panel depicts St John Baptiste De La Salle, with Rouen Cathedral behind him. Below he is seen in his classroom. The right panel pictures St Theresa, with the Basilica of Lisieux behind her, and below she is receiving roses from the Child Jesus. These lights recall the Grammar School the Canon caused to be founded, and the parish on the Manor he instigated. In the centre is his patron, St Oswald, King and Martyr, who is also the patron of the last parish and school he established—on the Wybourn. In the tracery above are the Device of the Christian Brothers, the Arms of St Oswald, and the Carmelite Shield. By chance, the feast of Sts Simon and Jude was also the Canon's ordination day.

THE NAVE

On the capitals of the pillars on the South aisle are various male saints (by custom, men used to sit in the benches on the right of the centre aisle, facing the High Altar)—St Gregory (Pope), St Cuthbert (Bishop), St Edward (King), St Paul (hermit), St Bede (monk), St Roche (pilgrim), and St Francis Xavier (missionary); and on the North aisle, female saints of various types—St Teresa (Abbess), St Bridget (nun), St Elizabeth of Hungary (Queen), St Monica (widow), St Catherine (Martyr), St Mary Magdalene (penitent), St Walburga (pilgrim), St Rose of Lima (Virgin).

The shields on the ceiling are the emblems of St Thomas More, St John Fisher and St Philip Howard, repeating the images in the first window of the North Wall. Around the walls are listed the names of the Forty Canonised English Martyrs. In the redecoration of 1988 the names of the Padley Martyrs on the Sanctuary Arch were altered from Ven. (Venerable) to Bl. (Blessed) Nicholas Garlick and Robert Ludlum, marking their beatification with their eighty-three companion martyrs in Rome in November 1987.

At the top of the Nave on the left hand pillar a marble tablet with inlaid brass cross is a memorial to a prominent citizen of Sheffield, Robert Gainsford who, fulfilling a long cherished wish to go to Rome, died there in 1870, aged 62. He is buried in Rome in the Church of St Laurence outside-the-walls.

On the westernmost pier of the south arcade of the nave is an alabaster and mosaic in memory of Charles Hadfield (1840-1916), son of the architect of the church, and architect of its Lady Chapel (1877-8) and of the Rectory (1903).

DIMENSIONS

Total length 43.75m (143ft. 7ins.)

Chancel length 11.63m (38ft. 2ins.)

Nave length 32.13m (105ft. 5ins.)

Nave width 7.51m (24ft. 8ins.)

North aisle width 5.48m (18ft. 0ins.)

South aisle width 5.18m (17ft. 0ins.)

Transept width 25.19m (82ft. 8ins.)

Height of Nave 15.80m (51ft. 10ins.)

Height of Chancel 14.73m (48ft. 4ins.)

Height of Tower to Parapet 28.11m (92ft. 3ins.)

Height of Spire to Cross 29.05m (95ft. 4ins.)

Height of Cross and Weather Vane 2.46m (8ft. 1in.)

Total height of Tower and Spire 59.62m (195ft. 8ins.)

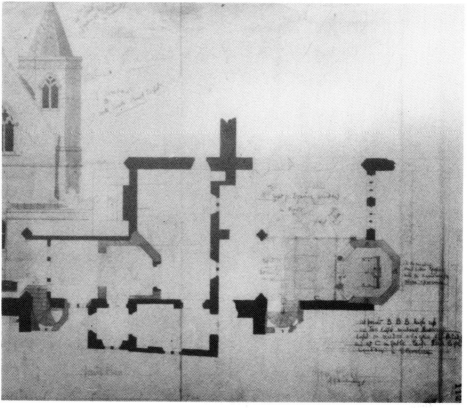